ROBERT KRUT is the author of *The Now Dark Sky, Setting Us All on Fire* (Codhill Press, 2019), which received the Codhill Poetry Award, *This Is the Ocean* (Bona Fide Books, 2013), and *The Spider Sermons* (BlazeVox, 2009). He lives in Los Angeles and teaches in the Writing Program and College of Creative Studies at the University of California, Santa Barbara.

ACKNOWLEDGMENTS

Thank you to the journals where the following poems initially appeared, or are forthcoming:

Air/Light: "Smoothing Stone"

The Bennington Review: "The Forest"

Birdcoat Quarterly: "Attempted Astronomy"

Clackamas Literary Review: "Collateral"

A Dozen Nothing: "The Branch"

Moria: "Corporate Intrigue" and "A Bar Called Nostalgia on Route 22"

Pine Hills Review: "365 X 365"

Radar: "The Anxious Lever of Lowering Sky"

Superstition Review: "Scream into an Open Mouth"

Watershed Review: "Watch Me Trick Ghosts," "You Are the Street, You Are the Sleep," and "Echolocation Manuscript"

8 Poems: "Shame Is the Chorus"

Thank you to the people who helped with many of these poems: Pete Miller, Trish Murphy, and Sarah Pape. Thanks to Mom, Dad, Keith, Emilie, Thomas, Eva, and the Bakers. Thank you to David Appelbaum, Susannah Appelbaum, James Sherwood, and Sophie Jeffries at Codhill—and, importantly, to Pauline Uchmanowicz, for bringing us together.

Love and special thanks to Sarah Baker.

THE FOREST

Grief turns us to trees,
the short finger of a branch
first pushing through a shoulder,
stretches out, rising above
your head, and then another,
growing outward from your side,
curls across your torso,
a bark-faced comma wrapping
your chest, and you are destined
to move everywhere with this awkward
armor, bumping into walls, lowering
yourself through doorways, hoping
this is it, that your eyes won't
turn to wooden spheres, your heart
to a ball of root, until you walk well
beyond the city, to a crowd of others,
leaf-wigged and motionless, each
meditating on the pinpoints of trees
holding up the draped sky, and they
welcome you, they welcome you.

ACCIDENTAL LIGHT

I'm walking after midnight,
I'm walking before sunrise,
investigating sirens
heard echoing off the bones
in the walls before
I walked out the door.

The only light comes from
the convenience store on the corner
that closed weeks ago,
their electricity still on,
the lottery sign glowing
against the glass that makes
the parking lot swell.

I'm walking alongside shadows
of no one, walking under
the dome curve of a pupil,
scanning for sound but only
finding a possum fighting
a raccoon behind an RV.

In the parking lot of the church
with a sign lit that just says
soon, a single sound calls out,
a car doing donuts, its headlights
off, the tires occasionally screaming
against the pavement
while it keeps circling, circling.

I'm walking long after midnight.
The scars of the world are turning neon.
I'm walking before sunrise.
Knocking on a stranger's door and running.

365 X 365

Every day is a finger, every week is a fist.
Friday is the devil's day, the devil is a day sleeper.
I'm counting down to see you.

If you're reading this, I'm talking to you.
No need to figure out the you in this calendar.
Hear my voice in your ears.

I hear yours.
Light a candle for dancing, watch shadows on the wall.
Shadowbox in preparation, you are concrete ballet.

I am concrete ballet.
My hands are cinder block, my feet are clouds.
Are you marking the days.

Mark the weeks with an X.
I've tattooed an X on my arm.
You've tattooed my name on your hand.

I am grasping your arm.
I don't feel it, do you feel it.
Each tooth is a tombstone, both eyes are a fuse.

My body is a calendar, your body is a calendar.
Monday is a new Monday, but you saw that coming.
I didn't.

We're wrapping in a circle, a loop of a piercing.
You are my earring, and you are my ear.
We are dancing.

YOU ARE A FORGOTTEN ANIMAL TOO

Inside the veins of a leaf's palm,
the heartbeat of root,
and inside the root, the syncopated

rhythm of a thousand grubs
pulsing beneath the dirt, and
below them, this alkaline margin

gives way to the broken-down bones
of animals long since extinct,
never pictured, never mythologized,

their dinosaur teeth jutting
from a human skull, alligator
torso held up by the legs of a bear,

buried in this spot before history,
before the seed that breathed
the tree that reaches out and up

to hold the sky from self-created
responsibility, a moot point while
we await our place among the obscure.

GRAVITY OF NUMBERS

Every day is a medicine ball to catch.
A helicopter circles overhead, tethered by its spotlight.
Good luck sleeping when heartbeats are drumming knives.
Ask the Lords of Gravity to reverse their ruling.
This undershirt weighs fifty pounds.
The first monarch of the season blinks onto a branch.
Fireworks go off in black and white further up the valley.
Make a list, erase a list, cook the list, eat the list.
Every vein is an unplugged wire with frayed ends.
A coffee cup on the sidewalk releases quarters like a slot machine.
Light is sound, sound is taste, and all is touch.
Every home is decorated in ribbon and polished for presentation.
When klieg lights turn horizontal, they split the horizon line.
Wash me in light, wash me in light.
A crowd disperses, runs in every direction through the houses.
Random patterns are still geometry.
Lift this coat of coal, breathe with forty lungs.
Silence is peace, silence is just a pause.
While a beetle climbs the doorjamb, looking for a way in.
You could lift this whole house over your head if you needed to.

GHOST DOES

Sky ghost prepares lightning.
Electricity ghost is acid on steel.
Thunder ghost speaks to tree ghost.
Tree ghost is you.
Foundation ghost stretches, contracts.
Wind ghost inhales.
Blanket ghost is bandaging.
Slate ghost marks in chalk.
Bone ghost is an echo.
Moon ghost is moon.
Sun ghost is moon ghost.
I am moon ghost.
Branch ghost is arm as body.
Rain ghost is a footprint on cement.
Leaf ghost lifts eyeline.
Tree ghost is waiting.
Tree ghost awaits.
Tree ghost is you.
I am tree ghost.
Tree ghost is moon ghost.
We hide, appear.

I have been scratching my knee
for fifteen minutes,
dug a parenthesis into dry skin.

Through the window and down
the street, a kid on a skateboard arcs
the pavement, moving like bass notes.

The board across the concrete
harmonizes with his movement,
the only sound in the block's shut mouth.

He's the last one alive,
he's the last one here,
and even a hungry animal

will let him pass.

AFTER THE CREDITS

Sitting in the front window, writing
in pantomime, studying
coffee's cream at 3 a.m.

If I stay here long enough,
the dry summer grass
will start to grow dew.

It is quiet, thank God,
so quiet out and in,
a muted TV flickering nearby.

I've written about the end
of the world so many times,
but realize:

I've written about the end of my
world, not the
world.

In daylight, I can't feel my feet
on the ground when I walk
through town.

Looking for food,
a rib-thin possum staggers
out of a shrub in the yard.

The house settles from years,
its 1930s body being pinched
by the invisible hand of a giant.

THE DIORAMA

Over this model of a town, your hand
drapes itself across rooftops, fingers
through alleys, the cobwebs that string
themselves like street lights,
their lace hung between corners.

The city is small now, and gives
to grids of light on its periphery,
while your cat claws at the cardboard
castles of skyscrapers. You blow dust
to the floor, a sort of practical purgatory,

empty space in the room beneath this
imagined town. There will be accidents
in these streets, but for now,
there are no people, no wax bodies
hardened in place. Only you, knowing

as well as anyone, if you don't see
the crowd, the crowd doesn't see you.

PUNCHLINE BEFORE SETUP

I repeat a joke
about myself
to a congregation of cocktail napkins
while the beams like bones
hold the ceiling in place,
the floor's cracked tile waits

for me as I hit the ground,
mistaken in thinking someone
will pick me up, prop me up
against a stool and ask
for my autobiography, until recognizing
the punchline, one they've heard before,

and they're right, of course,
and all the more reason why
we need to look after
each other, keep a stranger's
secrets, tell them only to the guy
at the bar with a beat-up briefcase,

who opens it like a mouth
to reveal a tape recorder
playing a loop of canned laughter
before walking out the door,
never to return, leaving it
in your greasepaint-covered hands.

PRAISE OUR PROTECTORS

Let our hands touch in sideways prayer,
let our breath synchronize on this beach,

and with an inhale, the sand will
turn to concrete beneath and around us,

baked by unhindered sun, tighter
and tighter into pavement until it cracks,

sea foam released through its revealed
fault lines, covering our feet and rising,

the ocean growing to fill in the world,
and we sit on its floor, a shark

passing with no interest, a whale
in the distance and far overhead—

look at me and I will look at you,
and swim through each other's pupils,

out through the other side where
we breathe underwater, and sand

is only sand, but the stars in the sky
are the eyes of deep sea creatures,

watching over us all.

NO FACE CAN READ THE HAWK

The degree to which we reconcile,
or try to do so,
is a hike across unmolded mountains,

bare feet on rocks, the great
farmers of sadness, dragging
the earth's knuckles on our journey,

until we approach a figure
standing at the canyon's edge who
turns then turns again, then

reaches out, its arm a branch
for the hawk that has risen
from the scar below

to claim its place, to claim
your face and move on for good,
as you know there is no choice

but to spend your life trying to write
this story and present it to all
who will listen as a letter

held between stones for those
who will find it and fly
long after we are gone.

THE BEGIN AGAIN ROOM

The door locks, the key breaks.
We are carved steel, but carved into what.
You're not going anywhere.
The room is a mile, the room is an inch.

The plumbing is frozen, the water is cloudy.
You breathe through a sliver in the window sill.
A swan curves the air outside, pulled by ribbon.
This is it now.

Put your palms to the wall.
The walls are moss, the room is a mouth.
The electric sockets exhale flower petals.
Ceiling is ice, the ceiling is clear.

The room is foliage, the walls are vine.
Your invitation is intrusion, now the room must begin again.
The water above trembles, waiting to be released.
You are a pile of metal filings, waiting for a magnet.

NAMING THE HOLIDAY

Driving a stolen car with my convicted
ghost twin, together we watch the sky
fold in on itself like a devil's cloak,

revealing ailing stars, celebrating
the anniversary of the death
of the world, trying

to create a name for this holiest
of holidays, but finding
no words exist

that do justice
to this need for sparklers
on the void's edge, to dance

on pavement opening itself
into earthquake anxiety,
to sing while watching

a dragon with a frantic chicken
in its fangs, merely an appetizer
before the meal,

until we drive away
listening to the oldies station,
since all stations are oldies stations

now, and look to each other's
faded faces and ask, *who* and *why*
but both of us

know the answers to each.

ATTEMPTED ASTRONOMY

It is his first day outside
and he will wear a suit.
He adjusts his tie in the bathroom mirror
only to notice his thumb nail
twitching until it shakes free
as the birthing wings of a beetle.

The half-moon insect now crawls
into the faucet before him. He moves
his gaze to the window where a breeze
makes the street's air gravity-less, clearing
away pollen. He expects to see a parade

but there is no one, no one, and
in the reflection, his hair is long, and
in the reflection, his beard is to his chest.
His hands are covered in dirt.

He turns on the water but it releases a spray
of minuscule flying insects—
beetles with the eyes of a fly,
spiders with wings of a dragonfly,
small praying mantis with centipede legs—
and they circle his head, a clueless
Saturn as he calls outside to no one
and stands in place like the dying planet he is.

ECHOLOCATION MANUSCRIPT

Snapping wood, scraping metal through the wall.
Initials scratched into the foundation with a blade.
What's in that room.

Dread isn't mystery it's anxiety and anxiety isn't entertainment.
The saw played like a violin sculpts a statue of an eyeless head.
What's in the walls.

Bones don't have identity.
The nerves are a short-circuiting power grid.
I don't know how to smile let alone mingle.

I know how to show my teeth when called for.
Is there a reason to now.
A snapshot by the lake is blackmail no matter who took it.

Humidity is a cloud of skin settling on the roof.
Electricity is veins and the house is sick.
The keys are locked under the floorboards.

The ceiling is a straitjacket for the door.
I donated my hand to the window sill.
What's in that room.

For months, a cloud has been pouring itself into our chimney.
A ghost with human texture reaches to tap us on the shoulders.
Footsteps across a bed of branches through the vents.

I have written a book about this sound.
I have written a book about this sound.
Then burned it.

THREE

FATE IS A FAITHFUL PAPERBACK ADAPTATION

The clock on the wall
pierces us to projection,
turning us to television, a broadcast
on the hand-me-down black and white

set propped up on a dinner table
where someone sits, one hand
holding a pen, the other covering
his eye, a face halfway invented,

trying to write a plot only
to find it's already been done,
while his plate of food gets cold,
the marbled meat turning to bone,

the photo negative of people
in the room shouting to look
up, look out the window
at the car careening down the street

with no driver, cruising in curves
until wrapping around the tree
in this very yard, out of focus
behind the screen, and

somewhere inside the cathode's
cold embrace, we take our bow.

an elaborate scaffolding of spider webs
tying the branch down, anchoring it in place—
beneath their tent, a hundred of them
shuffling along, tie it tightly, tightly—

rewarding themselves with a dinner
of trapped earwigs in the branch's finger.
So much web, it looks like
a cotton body, pulled apart

and laid to rest on the wood, and as
the sun lunges with its last rays
the whole contraption sparkles and
the spiders appear to disappear

and I stare
into that cloth diamond
until it is dark, and all movement
stops for the day,

and all I can think—
for that night and past—
will be how much I wish
I had taken you up there with me.

THE BRANCH

There is too much death and rain this year.
You would hope one would cancel
the other out, in some karmic double negative—
no such luck.

It has been pouring for a week,
and you've been dead for two days.
Today is Thursday, and finally, an arm
of sunlight holds back the storm.

The tree beside, above, and over
our building lost a branch and now
it's on the rooftop, rain matting its leaves
into a hundred shocked eyelids.

I stare at the phantom limb,
with clouds now just out to sea,
open mouths of water collected
in pavement pock marks.

The branch will stay there a week—
a great trophy big enough
to notice, not big enough
to warrant a rush removal.

By then, the branch
will have dried out long ago,
a chalky skeleton—the leaves, fossils
traced onto the floor, binding it all together—

A BAR CALLED NOSTALGIA ON ROUTE 22

Your hometown, like a photo negative
on top of a photo negative.

Standing outside the bar in the parking lot
of a strip mall, light a cigarette,
imagine it will taste like pine and winter air,
and instead, it just tastes like a cigarette.

Two old high school friends make out furiously
against the alley's back wall
while their respective families
sleep at home to the light of bedside laptops.

There is the temptation to treat
this whole town like a grave,
and the one woman dancing to
local cover band inside, its angel.

And that might make you tough, imagine
you are steel through brick,
but you are here, of course,
pulled by the gravity of habit and history.

The cigarette is done, and it wasn't even good.
The tree across the state road is a cell phone tower
disguised as an evergreen. Everyone is back inside
and the bass a muffled heartbeat through the walls.

Your hometown, a secret tattooed on your back,
never to be seen as you walk forward,
each step based on what you think
it says, and what you know it doesn't.

WE ALL SPY ON EACH OTHER

You sleep with your head
next to the plumbing, hear the couple
upstairs argue as inkblot staccato.

In the morning, they saw down
a dead tree, its bark falling
like forgotten language.

To get away from that sound, you
jump into the pool, beard chlorined
and bloodshot eyes, oblivious

to the crowd now gathered to set clear
cover over the water, roof of glass, lockdown
lens as you struggle.

You can only hear their voices
as vibrating cracks, can only see
their eyes as prismed stones

while they take notes and watch
you punch the glass
over and over and over and over.

NIGHT SHIFT AT CORNER CONVENIENCE

That was the summer I worked
midnight to eight, Tuesday through Sunday.

Each night, I dumped the soda machine
tray's run-off into the alley
because the place was a mess,
and keep it clean or you're fired.

Mid-July, a woman bought a pack of Camels,
methodically opened it in front of me
and slid one across the counter with a wink.
I slipped out back with a stolen lighter.

Through the crack in the door,
I saw two guys rush inside,
one smashing the lottery case with a bat,
the other holding a shotgun at the manager.

I dropped my smoke, and headed in
to I didn't know what,
or away from I didn't know what,

the bass snap of violence and the shouting
escalating into the alleyway
wind as the cigarette was carried across
the expanding lake of melted ice on pavement.

STREET FIGHT

Out here, I'm tagging a wall
with someone else's initials.

Punching concrete just leaves
skin on the pavement, chewing
gravel makes a gunpowder mouth.

And when I land a hit, my own eye
dyes itself purple,

when my knuckles connect
with a jaw, I spit out a tooth.

Don't tell me I'm free to do
what I want to do
when I want to do it

if I'm not the fist,
I am the wall.

CORPORATE INTRIGUE

The office park at dusk, a building
cleared out for a company closing, artifacts

stacked in the parking lot:
five fax machines lean
against twenty-five phones, their
cords intertwined
like the tails of a sleeping king rat.

I'm not making a shadow, standing
alone on the pavement.

The sun positions itself in setting
directly behind one streetlight,
the moon rising its face
just behind another.
I'm the only one here.

Everything is plastic in this
bulging monument, but for
one strand of hair, laced

through the curls of a phone cord,
a blonde thread that flutters
from wind, a last fabric of DNA.

I lean down, release it from the trap—
each of those phones start ringing—

the fax machine exhales a single sheet
that reads *who did this, where are we?*

PEDAGOGY

He wants to be a teacher, but what
to teach when the world is a tiger,

when even walking out to sneak a smoke
is met by a town where someone

behind a mailbox whips batteries
at unexpecting afternoon walkers,

where his jacket has the insignia
of a country he doesn't live in,

or at the very least one
where he no longer belongs,

and by the time the cigarette
has become a hand, the class

is on the street, searching
for who threw something at him,

their kindness
and its necessity crushing

as they lift the wedges of sidewalk,
leaving fingernails in concrete.

THE NEIGHBOR HANDS OUT
A PAMPHLET

The implication being that noise
equals bloodshed, which is a faulty
formula as we watch a fool
walk through the city, an invitation
in hand which he presses
between his lips then grinds
between his teeth and again
you tell yourself it's not
the end of the world but

he was welcomed here and now
your steps are crowded with paper
eating mannequins and you have no choice
but to accept the fact that
they are here to stay, formally invited
no less, the white noise of their chewing
and chants like so many black and white TVs
dragged out to their yards
by extension cords to light and
blind the neighborhood on command.

THE FURNACE

The house next door is all one room.
No one lives there.
The house next door is one big room.
A furnace in the center.

Last night, I walked in.
No one has lived there for years.
I'm telling you now, the scarred furnace was lit.
Inside, flames tethered to coals.

There was nothing on the walls.
Except a single painting of a painting:
a room with a furnace.
I am reporting back so you know.

I removed the painting to find a hole in the wall.
Copper wires humming a ghost harmony.
Your name was scratched into the picture frame.
I put the painting back.

The furnace inhaled its flames.
It went cold.
I walked out the door to no one.
I was on fire.

ON THE HOUSE'S HUNDREDTH BIRTHDAY

In the orange walls of a room
that holds a grudge,

we touch in sleep, hand across
leg, palm on waist.

The curtains release a thin
veil of ghosts

who trace our bodies
with a hundred fingertips.

The candlestick's wax
like a bloody fungus remains

while the wick curls
to light itself and reveal

newspaper clippings
beneath the wallpaper

that will last long
after we have moved on.

The thumb of an air bubble working
its way under the surface for years.

COLLATERAL

He says a prayer for the first time in years,
about the heart of the world being ripped out,

begging for a sun to fill that open-wound-
earth-core, then waits—

and that night, every manhole downtown
bursts from the pavement, flies upward

atop columns of light shot from each,
holy cylinders, luminary towers

stopping the city on sight, and the city
stands in awe, rinsed in the glow—

while he holds onto his secret at first
out of humility, until

one by one, people walk
to these great and blessed tubes,

reaching hands into their illumination,
then step fully into the light, above

the perfect circle mouth, and they
float, it seems, for a moment,

for a moment without gravity, held
by some hand of divine compassion

before dropping like so much mindless
meat to the great, gray-watered

Lethe that still moves below,
and *I'm sorry, I'm sorry.*

THE BLOOD OF HUMAN KINDNESS

This savory sunset brings out all
the habitual parade goers, blocks
of the city's finest amblers,
a dance of bones just beneath
the skin's veiled surface, where
an old-timer clasps both sides when shaking
hands, offers an orange with a smile,
the shroud of human decency hiding
the harm awaiting, the teeth
blossoming from his spine, the fingernails
growing from his skull like tiled horns,
and to take even a morsel of that food
reveals the X-ray of this whole scene,
that it's not a celebration, it's a feeding.

THE ANXIOUS LEVER
OF LOWERING SKY

Fear is a blade held in a lung.
The sky lowers an inch each night.

Play pinfinger till dawn, you have ten.
Keep sticking your thumb in a socket.
Electrical or eye it's all the same.

You walk through the room like an aspirin.
Sleep is pointless when day is night.
A lump of ground rises to make your sofa.

When you breathe, you create the clouds.
The clouds are a loose brain of lightning.
That is not something to celebrate.

You did all of this and nothing, take credit, or don't.
Eat praise like porridge, drink anger like poison.
Both leave you full, exhaling sky.

A knock at the door, but the moon
covers your mouth like a mask.

TWO

WATCH ME TRICK GHOSTS

It helps to become wind, move
like air while a sheet of their thousand
misshapen eyes floats beside you.

It helps to make regret a small
paper house, a barroom matchbook
inside, waiting to light.

It helps to climb on top
of the bookcase, just out of the sight
line of their ever-changing faces.

It helps to make memory a cape, drape
it across your shoulders, feel
it curl to ash against skin.

It helps to become water, let
them set their sins on your surface,
sail across and past.

It helps to stand outside the window, see
each exhale themselves, wait
to steal your breath, but

watch me trick ghosts
and leave the house, hollow and free.

YOU ARE THE STREET,
YOU ARE THE SLEEP

Here is a steel seed.
Place it on your chest before you go to sleep.
Wake with filings across your eyelids.

Each dream, a capsule riding your bloodstream.
Rest in a cocoon wrapped with steel wool.
Let red lines mark your arms in maps.

Go get a cup of coffee.
Cough at the sink, trace your blue light.
Pull wire floss from your molars.

Outside the window, someone in motion.
Etching a name into a street sign pole with a knife.
There is no sound tonight.

You will try to sleep again.
The pipes in the house snapping their elbows.
You attempt water, you settle for metal.

Sell your books at World of Books!
Go to sell.worldofbooks.com and get an instant price quote. We even pay the shipping - see what your old books are worth today!

Inspected By: eduard_zawadi

FROM THE ROOF AT NIGHT

Couldn't sleep so I climbed to the roof—
sitting on the angle, waiting
for the sun to rise.

Every roof a coffin cover
for the neighboring dreams
that plagiarize sadness.

There is no sound, really, just
the attempt to balance and shift
my palms against the tile's cold slate.

I want this silence.
I want to see the sun come up
in curved horizontal margins.

Down the block, someone
walks between the street-side trees
with their head wrapped in duct tape.

I zero in on the sky, position
my gaze to the directional
line of the incoming light,

awaiting the honey yolk
of early morning across the city,
its ribbon of blood inside.

Against the chimney,
the remnants of a bird's nest,
a chewed and scattered bowl.

SERPENTINE ARITHMETIC

The desk lamp interrogates
the sheet of graph paper
where he calculates the percentage
of truth in each lie he's told
as well as each falsehood
spoken in return.

His math is faulty and the formulas
are flawed, no number what he expects
as the pencil wears down to a dull
knuckle of lead and the phone rings,

a call from the Minister of monitors,
who says, *listen, listen*
I'll only say this once—

the window turns to stained glass
embedded with data,
the silhouette of a snake
pushes itself up the surface
outside, its shadowed curves
gravity-less, leaving

a vertical line of statistics
in its trail for someone to decipher—

but not him, as he writes
each of his stories in a ledger, only
to set it on the sill, wait
for that creature to
circle it, strangle it, and move on.

TOURNIQUET ROAD

We return from the road when the road
turned bone and the gas stations all
rib cages. You are a heart,
which is different from saying
you are my heart or you have my
heart. It is saying that
you are a heart.

The sound of street lamps throb
when we speak under the city's
drumbeats. You can whisper, I
can hear. I'll lower my voice until
merely impersonating speech,
and your lips, soft Morse code. Everyone
is watching. No one is watching.

When this is all over, and the buildings
boarded up, I'll be here,
watching for you, after
an embrace as windows smash
themselves out, their shards on the road
leading the way
like a vein to a wound.

MAGIC'S BITTER COCKTAIL

Beware the welcome mat
at nature's gate, the yard's elbowed
branch that holds five lanterns, swayed
by hidden fingers of a ghost, beware

the pathway where bark masks the naked
torsos of those who came before, where
all human voices turn to echo, then
whisper, then sonic dust blowing

to the feet of the alchemist and the treasurer,
who barter before a vat
bubbling with your memory, waiting
to pour it into glass bottles for mass

consumption without your knowledge, and
no one will know your name but they
will know what you've done, or
haven't, while you crawl

to a corner trying to take pride
in the simple act of getting
old, of making it through other calendars,
through somber years meant for magic.

SHAME IS THE CHORUS

This year's crop is all huskless corn,
this year's scrapes never turn to scabs,
this year's skin is a rope burn tattoo.

Wherever you are, raise champagne
to time passing, this calendar
a voucher for certain celebration.

Down the road, a revival's Bibles
are hollowed out to hide knives,
and the congregation won't handle snakes.

Don't trust that preacher's promise of cold
bottled water, of giant fans cooling
the crowd and their sweat-veil faces.

Meditate on the tree line in your yard,
wave to the ghosts snagged in branches
like balloons as they watch in judgment.

They do not show weakness,
and in a moment three days
to the left and three nights to the north,

each screams shame
into the wind that slams against our windows,
waking us in the middle of the night.

WALK DON'T WALK
WALK STAND STILL

Letters from leper street signs
fall to the pavement before us,
cursive S the size of a body

drops, hits the ground
and clangs in ignored echoes.
We don't even comment anymore.

Everyone walks the city
like the innermost body
of a Russian nesting doll,

chipped with cracks like thin
lightning along their skulls, the passing
cabs rattling their delicate woodwork.

How do you even speak
when everyone is about to fall apart
all the time and every day?

At the corner, the traffic stop
lights an unknown glyph,
a circle pierced by four arrows,

and we stand together, unaware
the sky will become collapsing
concrete, turn this all to dust, and

start fresh with us nothing
more than powder
for new clay.

A COFFIN IS A BATTERY

A ball of wires, wrapped in a fist.
A wrist of ropes, arm of electricity.
Ambiguity is a lock and ether is steel.
Feel the rods bend to radiation.

Watch this trick: I'm locked in a coffin.
Often the trap is the trick and that is that.
Facts are grubs in a dirt maze.
What stays in the ground is public domain.

Who am I kidding, you punch your way out.
Subtlety is a gift for the privileged.
Edges must be splintered, not smoothed.
Thundered walls make rooms of light.

All of the town draped in power lines.
Fine hairs of stray electricity twitch in wind.
Next to shards of wood, I stand barefoot.
When you come looking, I am the wires.

THIS MEMOIR IS A DEVIL'S DEAL

My ghostwriter stares with pentagram pupils,
scanning for a tell, waiting for the slip
when my eyelid twitches, when my tongue
circles an incisor in my silent mouth,

when I admit, off the record, that it is all my fault,
this whole petty and awful operation.
Can we write a book about how a prayer
released columns of burning light across the city?

Can this be one final attempt to take
responsibility as if it were only a confession
to simply sign and fold
into the pages of my autobiography,

the corner scented with the smell of burnt
paper, scaled by sun, and my handwriting:
the world gets the demon we deserve,
a smug final assessment.

And my conversation partner
leans in, embracing me
in crimson light, to say
you
not we,

you.

GIVE UP

Melancholy is the cartilage
of this summer's body.

There is a lack of wind
at one a.m., the doors open,

a spider in the frame giving up
on its web, suspended mid-air.

The same guy walks past
the house every night at midnight,

slumped shoulders and holding
the leash to an oblivious poodle,

that sweet dog strutting along despite
its anchor being

this breathing corpse who heads every night
to the corner convenience

to see if they have changed
their hours deeper into the night, despite

a handwritten note to the contrary.
The dog's fascination

with the mystery of the sidewalk shrub
is enough to make its owner pause,

tilt his head upward, caught
in the moon's heroin, raise

a hand hello and then return
to August's unwashed undershirt.

SMOOTHING STONE

In the river it is always night.
Lay flat, breathe by drowning.
Under the water, you can't see the land on fire.
Become the river's lung.

Don't say a prayer, become a prayer.
Lower yourself without help.
There is no gravity inside the river.
Each pebble is another moon.

There is moss, there is a blanket for rest.
The river is dark and the river is cold.
Each pebble beneath you cools the hillside heat.
Understand this bed levitates.

A water snake curls across your torso.
You are an animal, a creature who inhales water.
Your fingers are ten parades of pebbles.
Drown your hands under the water and silt.

The fire is without gravity, it is hair in wind.
It inhales you, it exhales you.
Stay still, and drink the water with your lungs.
Smoke is reflected on the river, smoke reflects the river.

It is always night in the river.
It pulls you to its mouth, the moon's mouth.
A pebble in your pocket, your skull smoothed by water.
You are stone and you are current.

SCREAM INTO AN OPEN MOUTH

My torso is crowded.
My body grew another heart
to house my rage.

An old man sells hand rolled cigarettes
in an abandoned grocery's parking lot,
a handwritten sign says
if you smoked, you'd be home now,
until two cops pay a visit.

My hands are packed houses.
I woke up with six fingers on each.
Every finger has four knuckles.

At the gas station up the street,
a guy walks up
to each pump, licks every handle
and walks away.

My organs have rerouted all
mechanisms, as bile turns to teardrops,
saliva becomes blood.

Two people stand on the corner
in front of my very home, screaming
directly into each other's mouths.
Pausing, they gesture, *yes,*
we know. Don't you?

My body grew an extra heart
to house my rage.

THE DINNER PARTY

All the conversations tonight are about wounds.
What a kind nicety to be tired of talking about wounds.
The wine glasses each have a fingertip in their bowl.

The wounds are described at length.
Looking for an exit, only entrances.
Looking for an entrance, only a wound.

You learned how to give stitches when you were just thirteen.
To yourself, lost in the woods on a camping trip.
The teacher found you, poured alcohol on the suturing.

Raise a toast to memory, raise a glass of fingers.
The table is a boat on an ocean of sighs and then laughter.
Some of the wounds look like a mouth.

The entrance is a window, the window is a ladder.
The host leads a prayer to our wounds.
Everyone is served a plate of teeth.

The laughter is a blade held in your side for safekeeping.
Stand up, stand up and share your wounds.
Or leave the party with a tourniquet and a missing limb.

ONE

"While overhead on its iron grill / Somebody's shape a sheet / Unwinds from slowly tosses in our moonless heat."
—James Merrill, "Walking All Night"

". . . The river is so small now // It will be hard to drown / In it. And still this world's a pretty one. // What world."
—Lucie Brock-Broido, "Herculaneum"

We All Spy On Each Other	31
A Bar Called Nostalgia on Route 22	32
The Branch	33
Fate Is a Faithful Paperback Adaptation	35

THREE

Echolocation Manuscript	39
Attempted Astronomy	40
Naming the Holiday	41
The Begin Again Room	42
No Face Can Read the Hawk	43
Praise Our Protectors	44
Punchline Before Set Up	45
The Diorama	46
After the Credits	47
Ghost Does	49
Gravity of Numbers	50
You Are a Forgotten Animal Too	51
365 X 365	52
Accidental Light	53
The Forest	54

CONTENTS

ONE

The Dinner Party	5
Scream into an Open Mouth	6
Smoothing Stone	7
Give Up	8
This Memoir Is a Devil's Deal	9
A Coffin Is a Battery	10
Walk Don't Walk Walk Stand Still	11
Shame Is the Chorus	12
Magic's Bitter Cocktail	13
Tourniquet Road	14
Serpentine Arithmetic	15
From the Roof at Night	16
You Are the Street, You Are the Sleep	17
Watch Me Trick Ghosts	18

TWO

The Anxious Lever of Lowering Sky	21
The Blood of Human Kindness	22
Collateral	23
On the House's Hundredth Birthday	24
The Furnace	25
The Neighbor Hands Out a Pamphlet	26
Pedagogy	27
Corporate Intrigue	28
Street Fight	29
Night Shift at Corner Convenience	30

CODHILL
PRESS

Codhill books are published by
David Appelbaum for Codhill Press

codhill.com

WATCH ME TRICK GHOSTS
Copyright © 2021 Robert Krut

All rights reserved under International and
Pan-American copyright conventions. First Edition.

Published in the United States of America

ISBN 978-1-949933-13-0

Cover and Book Design by Jana Potashnik
BAIRDesign, Inc. · bairdesign.com

Cover Painting by Pablo Prado

WATCH
ME
TRICK
GHOSTS

POEMS

ROBERT KRUT

CODHILL PRESS
NEW YORK · NEW PALTZ

ALSO BY ROBERT KRUT

The Now Dark Sky, Setting Us All on Fire
This Is the Ocean
The Spider Sermons

WATCH
ME
TRICK
GHOSTS